A TRUE BOOK™

D0686015

The Food Pyramid

CHRISTINE TAYLOR-BUTLER

Children's Press®
An Imprint of Scholastic Inc.
New York   Toronto   London   Auckland   Sydney
Mexico City   New Delhi   Hong Kong
Danbury, Connecticut

Content Consultant

Lawrence J. Cheskin, M.D., F.A.C.P.
Director, Johns Hopkins Weight Management Center
The Johns Hopkins University
Baltimore, Maryland

Library of Congress Cataloging-in-Publication Data

Taylor-Butler, Christine.
  The Food Pyramid / by Christine Taylor-Butler.
        p. cm. -- (A true book)
  Includes index.
      ISBN-13: 978-0-531-16859-2 (lib. bdg.)
                978-0-531-20733-8 (pbk.)
      ISBN-10: 0-531-16859-X (lib. bdg.)
                0-531-20733-1 (pbk.)

 1. Food--Juvenile literature. 2. Nutrition--Juvenile literature.
I. Title. II. Series.

TX355.T39 2008
641.3--dc22   2007036017

No part of this publication may be reproduced in whole or in part, or stored in a retrieval system, or transmitted in any form or by any means, electronic, mechanical, photocopying, recording, or otherwise, without written permission of the publisher. For information regarding permission, write to Scholastic Inc., 557 Broadway, New York, NY 10012.

Produced by Weldon Owen Education Inc

©2008 Scholastic Inc.

All rights reserved. Published in 2008 by Children's Press, an imprint of Scholastic Inc.
Published simultaneously in Canada. Printed in China. 62
SCHOLASTIC, CHILDREN'S PRESS, A TRUE BOOK, and associated logos are trademarks and/or registered trademarks of Scholastic Inc.

2 3 4 5 6 7 8 9 10 R 17 16 15 14 13 12 11 10 09 08

Find the Truth!

Everything you are about to read is true *except* for one of the sentences on this page.

Which one is **TRUE**?

T or F Exercise is part of the food pyramid.

T or F The number of obese children has declined in the past 20 years.

Find the answers in this book.

Contents

THE BIG TRUTH!

Healthy Eating Around the World

Milk, cheese, and yogurt help build strong bones.

4 Health and the Pyramid

Why is iron so important? 35

5 Making Choices Count

How many steps does the average person take in a day? 39

Eating sugary foods for breakfast gives you a quick energy boost. But it soon wears off. You are left feeling tired.

CHAPTER 1

An Energy Boost

Today, you have a big test at school. You get up early to start the day. Your mother suggests oatmeal and raisins with low-fat milk for breakfast. Instead, you eat a large bowl of your favorite sugar-coated cereal. The box says it will give you an instant energy boost. How long will that energy boost last?

Breakfast provides you with energy to start the day.

There's one small problem. Your test is not
until the afternoon. By lunch, you're hungry again.
You've already used up the energy from the sugary
cereal. In fact, you're so hungry that you have
a big helping of macaroni and cheese. You even
have seconds.

By the time you have to take your test, you feel very tired. You have trouble concentrating on your work. What's going on?

You ate plenty of **calories**. But they were not the right kind. Foods high in sugar, such as your cereal, and some other **carbohydrates**, such as macaroni, are absorbed into your system quickly. You get a quick burst of energy. Then you start to crash when the energy has been used up.

Fruit can be fresh, canned, frozen, dried, or squeezed.

Fruit makes an ideal snack. However, go easy on fruit juice. Some brands contain added sugar.

It would have been better to fill your plate with calories that count. It is important to eat the right quantities of food. It is also important to choose the right kinds of food to eat each day. When combined with exercise, these foods will keep you alert. They will keep your body working properly all day long.

Fitness is an important part of some school programs.

Supersize

Watch what you eat. Watch how much you eat too. Supersized fast-food meals may look delicious. However, they may contain enough calories for a whole day! A child who is between eight and twelve years old needs between 1,600 and 2,200 calories each day.

A supersized fast-food meal might consist of a cheeseburger, a large order of fries, and a triple-thick chocolate shake. That is the recommended calorie intake for a whole day. Many fast-food restaurants now offer healthier options. These include salads, fruit slices, milk-based drinks, and water.

The first U.S. food pyramid had five major food groups. Fats, oils, and sweets were at the tip of the pyramid.

CHAPTER 2

The Food Pyramid

The sweets at the tip of the pyramid provide little nutritional value.

The food pyramid is a guide to what to eat each day. The first U.S. food pyramid was created in 1992. It helped people understand how to eat wisely. In 2005, the U.S. food pyramid was changed. More information was added. The new pyramid also includes exercise.

Building a Pyramid for All

The first U.S. food pyramid had horizontal layers and pictures of food. That made it easy to understand. People were supposed to eat more of the foods at the bottom of the pyramid. They were supposed to eat less of the foods at the top. The pyramid recommended eating a variety of foods. It suggested eating plenty of grain products, vegetables, and fruits. Fats, oils, and sweets were to be eaten sparingly. The 1992 pyramid was an attempt to have one food guide for all people.

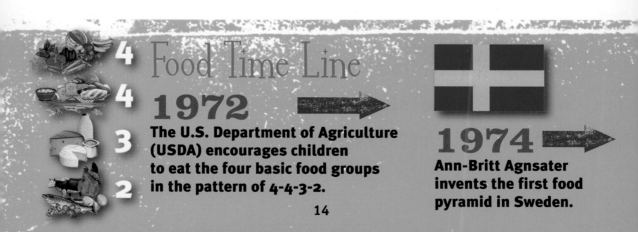

4
4
3
2

Food Time Line

1972 ➡️
The U.S. Department of Agriculture (USDA) encourages children to eat the four basic food groups in the pattern of 4-4-3-2.

1974 ➡️
Ann-Britt Agnsater invents the first food pyramid in Sweden.

The first U.S. pyramid was intended to help people choose a healthful diet. However, many experts found the pyramid too rigid. They also felt it was not clear enough about the serving sizes. These critics claimed that the recommended servings and calorie intake could not be the same for everyone. Today, the food pyramid has twelve different models. These vary with a person's age, gender, and activity level. The pyramid is very adaptable. That is why it is also known as MyPyramid.

1992
The USDA creates the first U.S. food pyramid.

2005
The USDA redesigns the U.S. food pyramid. It now includes exercise.

The New Pyramid

The new pyramid has six vertical stripes. Wide stripes mean to eat more servings of a food group. Narrow stripes mean to eat less. Each color starts out thin at the top of the pyramid. It gets thicker near the bottom. This reminds people that not all foods in a group should be eaten in the same amount. For instance, you should drink lots of milk. However, you should eat only a little ice cream.

Each color in the food pyramid is for a specific food group. Oils make up the yellow stripe. It is the thinnest stripe. Only a small amount is needed.

Grains

**Examples of
One Serving**
- 1 slice of bread
- 1 cup of cereal
- ½ cup of vegetables
- 1 piece of fruit
- 1 cup of milk or yogurt
- 1 ½ ounces of cheese
- 2–3 ounces of cooked meat
- 1 egg

The new pyramid has another feature that the old pyramid did not have. It has a staircase. That shows you that exercise is also a big part of a healthful lifestyle.

Vegetables   Fruits   Oils   Milk   Meat and beans

MILK

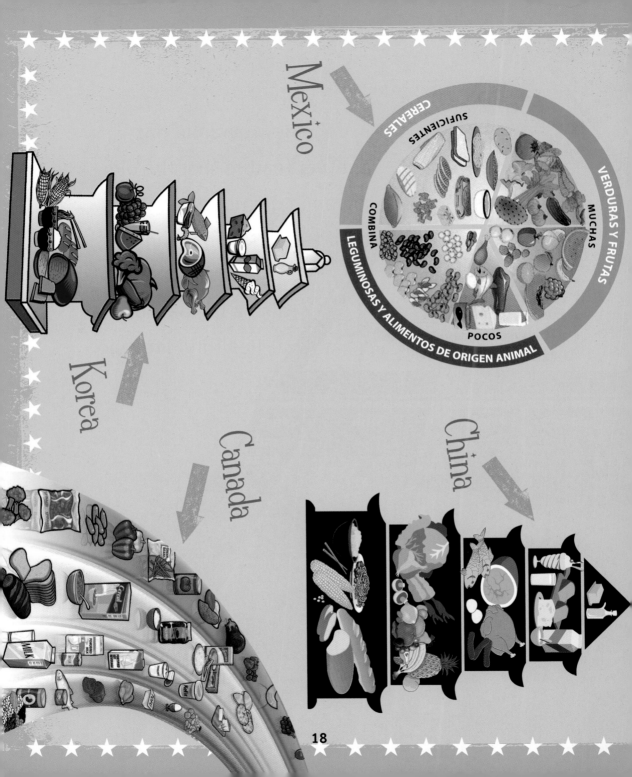

Mexico

Korea

Canada

China

CEREALES
SUFICIENTES
VERDURAS Y FRUTAS
MUCHAS
POCOS
COMBINA
LEGUMINOSAS Y ALIMENTOS DE ORIGEN ANIMAL

MILK

18

Healthy Eating Around the World

The first food pyramid was created in Sweden in 1974. In other parts of the world, there are food wheels, food maps, and food pagodas. It doesn't matter what the style is. The purpose is the same. It is to help people make the best food choices.

Swedish Food Pyramid (1974)

19

RED CLUSTER
TOMATOES

20

CHAPTER 3

The Pyramid Colors

Vegetables and fruits are full of **fiber**. Fiber helps food move through the intestines.

The food pyramid is not a diet plan. It is a guide that helps you choose a variety of healthful foods each day. It also helps you get the most nutrition out of the foods that you eat. The choices you make each day may affect your health for a long time.

Orange Stripe: Make Half Your Grains Whole

Grains are the seeds of wheat, corn, rice, and other cereal plants. They make up the pyramid's widest stripe. People should eat lots of grains. Grains are rich in carbohydrates. These are starches and sugars. The body converts these into energy.

Grains are often processed into flour. Many of the grains in cereals and breads have been refined. The tough outer coverings of the grains are removed. The processing removes some of the fiber, iron, and vitamin B.

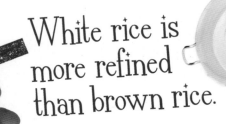

White rice is more refined than brown rice.

The new food pyramid suggests that you get half of your daily grain intake from whole grains. Whole grains contain all parts of the seeds, or kernels. These are the bran, germ, and endosperm. Foods made with whole grains are absorbed by your body more slowly. They provide you with a steady source of energy throughout the day. The fiber in whole grains helps foods move through your digestive system more quickly than refined grains.

Cross Section of a Wheat Seed

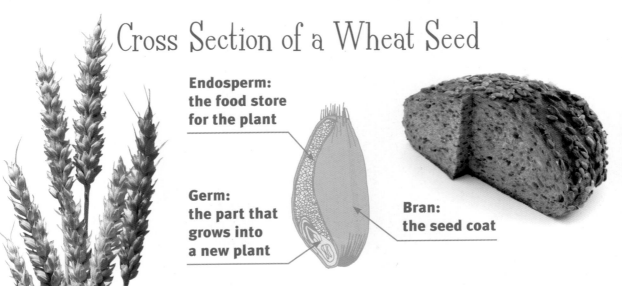

Endosperm: the food store for the plant

Germ: the part that grows into a new plant

Bran: the seed coat

Green Stripe: Vary Your Veggies

Vegetables are nutritious. They are high in fiber. They are also high in vitamins and minerals. They are low in fat and calories. Vegetables can help your eyesight and keep your skin healthy. They can lower blood pressure. They can decrease the likelihood of heart disease. They can even help protect against some forms of cancer.

Many experts suggest that you eat plenty of orange and dark-green vegetables.

Orange vegetables contain vitamin A and carotenoids. These are healthy for your heart, skin, and eyesight. They are also good for your overall immunity.

It is good to eat about 2 ½ cups of vegetables every day. The food pyramid suggests that you vary your vegetables. You should eat more than one color a day.

Red Stripe: Focus on Fruits

The USDA calls fruit "Nature's treat—sweet and delicious." Fruit is full of vitamins and carbohydrates. Citrus fruit, such as oranges, is full of vitamin C. This is essential for healthy bones and teeth. Fruit contains a lot of water too. This provides fluid for the body. Fruit is also low in fat and salt.

The word *fruit* comes from a Latin word meaning "enjoy."

Food Value of a Banana

CARBOHYDRATES
22.2%

WATER
75.7%

PROTEIN
1.1%

FAT
0.2%

OTHER
0.8%

CALORIES
ABOUT **100**

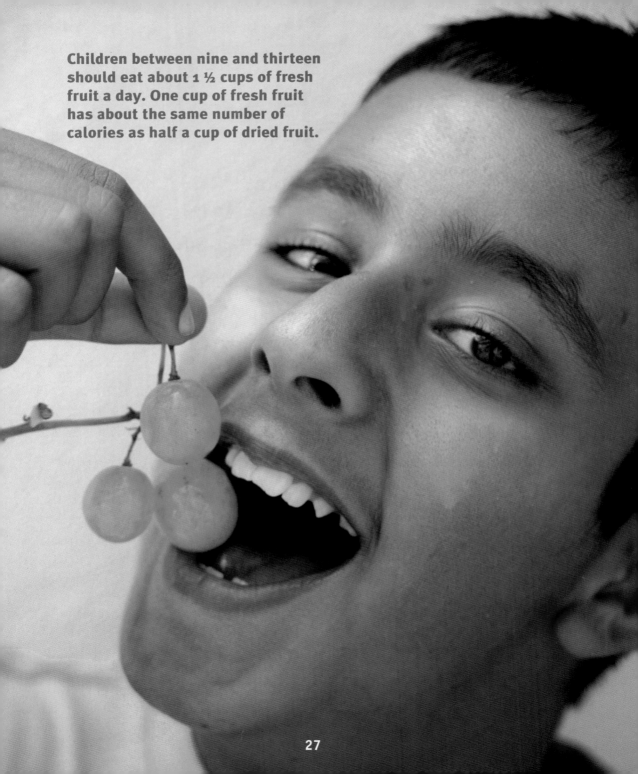

Children between nine and thirteen should eat about 1 ½ cups of fresh fruit a day. One cup of fresh fruit has about the same number of calories as half a cup of dried fruit.

Blue Stripe: Get Your Calcium-Rich Foods

Milk contains **calcium** and vitamin D. It helps build strong bones. The body uses vitamin D to help transport calcium to your bones. Milk and yogurt are often fortified with both ingredients. This means that extra calcium and vitamins are added during processing.

Some people are allergic to milk products. Many cereals and orange juices are now fortified with vitamin D and calcium.

Low-fat or fat-free milk products are usually a better choice than whole milk.

The fat in one glass of whole milk equals about four strips of bacon!

All dairy products contain calcium. However, some dairy products, such as cheeses, also have a high fat content.

Purple Stripe: Go Lean With Protein

Meat, poultry, fish, eggs, beans, nuts, and seeds are in the purple stripe. They are good sources of **protein** and vitamins. They also contain minerals. The minerals include iron, magnesium, and zinc.

Proteins are the body's building material. Skin, muscles, and hair are mainly protein. Foods rich in vitamin C help your body absorb iron. Iron carries oxygen in the blood. Magnesium helps release energy from your muscles. Zinc helps your immune system work properly.

Beans belong to the pea family. They are a good substitute for meat. They are high in protein.

Some foods in the purple group also contain fats and **cholesterol**. The food pyramid suggests that you go lean with protein. This means try to choose lean or low-fat meats and poultry.

Cholesterol is a fatty substance. Poultry and fish are lower in cholesterol than red meat. Grilling meat helps remove excess fats.

Yellow Stripe: Change Your Oil

Oils are not a food group. However, small amounts each day are essential for your health. You can get a daily supply by eating foods such as fish and nuts. Or you can add small amounts to your food when cooking. Oils from animal fats are high in cholesterol. Vegetable-based oils are better choices. These include olive, corn, soybean, or canola oil.

Cholesterol is found only in foods from animal sources.

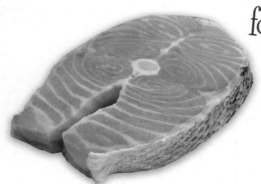

Cold-water fish, such as salmon, are full of heart-healthy omega-3 oils.

Climb the Steps

By exercising daily or almost daily, you can help your body use up the calories you eat. Exercise helps you maintain a healthy weight. It keeps your bones and muscles in good shape. When you exercise, your heart and lungs grow stronger. You are able to supply your body with more energy when you need it.

The food pyramid suggests that children should be physically active for at least 60 minutes on most days.

Water is important to good health.
Your body gets water from
foods as well as liquids.
Water helps your body
remove waste material.

CHAPTER **4**

Health and the Pyramid

By choosing certain foods, you can help your health. For instance, eating foods that contain fiber will help your body get rid of waste material. Oils found in certain fish improve heart and brain function. Foods rich in vitamin A, such as carrots and pumpkins, help improve your eyesight.

 It can be unhealthy to drink too much water. Thirst is the best indicator of your need for water.

35

Diabetes

Your cells depend on energy to survive. This energy comes from glucose. Glucose is a sugar derived from many of the foods you eat. It is absorbed into your cells with the help of **insulin**. Insulin is a **hormone**.

Diabetes is a disease in which a person's body produces too little insulin or uses it ineffectively. People with diabetes cannot properly absorb sugars. They must continually monitor and adjust their blood-sugar levels. Exercise and healthy eating can help regulate blood sugar. They can also lower a person's risk of getting diabetes.

Glucose meters help people with diabetes check their blood-sugar levels. Many people with diabetes also carry insulin with them.

Anemia

Iron helps red blood cells carry oxygen to the rest of the body. Oxygen helps the body turn glucose into fuel that it can use. Lack of iron may cause a condition called **anemia**. The word *anemia* means "without blood."

People with anemia feel tired. They find it difficult to concentrate. They need to eat foods that are rich in iron. People with anemia should never treat themselves for the condition. Iron is important. However, too much iron can be dangerous. It could make you sick. It could even kill you.

Lean meat, lentils, beans, and green leafy vegetables, such as spinach, are high in iron.

A pedometer
(peh-DAH-muh-tur)
records the number
of steps a person takes
as he or she walks.
Exercise burns
calories.

Pedometer

CHAPTER 5

Making Choices Count

Food provides your body with energy. A unit of energy is called a calorie. The food pyramid suggests the number of calories to eat each day. It shows you healthy ways to get those calories. Stay within your daily calorie needs. Otherwise, you may gain or lose weight. The number of obese children has more than doubled in the past 20 years.

On average, a person takes about 5,300 steps a day. Fitness experts recommend you take at least 10,000 steps.

It's All About Balance

Being an average weight for your age is good for your overall well-being. Maintaining that weight is a matter of balance. The energy you take in as food and drink should match the energy you burn off. If you eat 100 calories more each day than you burn, you'll gain about one pound per month.

Limit the amount of refined sugar you eat. Refined sugar is often found in desserts or packaged foods with added sugar. Sugar hides under names such as glucose, sucrose, and fructose. Skip the soda. It's full of sugar and calories. It has almost no nutritional value.

There are about 155 calories in a 12-ounce can of soda.

Nutrition Facts

Labels on food and drink packages list the number of calories the product contains. The USDA requires companies to list important nutrition facts on food labels too. This helps you keep track of what you are eating. Look for the healthful ingredients. These include vitamins, minerals, and calcium. Watch out for large amounts of ingredients that are not healthful. These include fat, sodium, and cholesterol.

The label tells you what the serving size is. It tells you how many servings are in the package. It will also show you how much of the average daily requirement you are eating with each serving.

Nutrition Facts

Serving Size 1 cup (252g)
Servings Per Container about 2

Amount Per Serving

Calories 270	Calories from Fat 70

	% Daily Value*
Total Fat 7g	11%
Saturated Fat 2.5g	13%
Trans Fat 0g	
Cholesterol 15mg	5%
Sodium 1310mg	54%
Total Carbohydrate 43g	14%
Dietary Fiber 2g	6%
Sugars 9g	
Protein 9g	

Vitamin A 10%	•	Vitamin C 0%
Calcium 2%	•	Iron 10%

* Percent Daily Values are based on a 2,000 calorie diet.

INGREDIENTS: WATER, TOMATO PASTE, FLOUR (WHEAT FLOUR, NIACIN, MONONITRATE, RIBOFLAVIN), BEEF, HIGH FRUCTOSE CORN MEAL (WHEAT FLOUR, NIACIN, CORN STARCH, SALT, TEXTURED PROTEIN (SOY FLOUR CARMEL), URAL FLAVOR, SEASONING, LYZED CORN AND SOY PROTEIN, LYZED CORN GLUTEN WITH NIACIN, ONION POWDER, CITRIC ACID, GLUTAMATE, CARAMEL COLOR, FIED CHEESE (CHEDDAR CHEESE CHEESE CULTURES, SALT), SALT, DISODIUM PHOSPHATE, RIKA, OLEORESIN CARMEL CONTAINS: WHEAT, SOY, MILK

212 22 0137 REAL

0 85239

Get Out and Move

Exercise is an important part of your day. The best exercise is the type that gets your heart beating faster. Try walking briskly or playing a game of basketball. Swimming, bicycling, and dancing count too. Even doing yard work burns calories. It gives your body a workout.

Best of all, exercise combined with eating right will make you feel better. Your body will function better and for a longer time. That's what the food pyramid is all about! ★

Year food pyramid revised: 2005

Recommended amount of daily exercise for children: 60 minutes every day, or on most days

Percentage of children who exercise at least one day a week: About 77 percent

Average recommended calories each day: About 2,200 for teen girls; 2,500 for teen boys

Percentage of overweight U.S. children (6–19 years): About 34 percent

Number of calories in a small order of French fries: About 209

Number of calories burned in a 30-minute brisk walk: About 100 calories

Did you find the truth?

T Exercise is part of the food pyramid.

F The number of obese children has declined in the past 20 years.

Resources

Books

Barron, Rex. *Showdown at the Food Pyramid*. New York: Putnam Juvenile, 2004.

DK Publishing. *My Food Pyramid*. New York: DK Children, 2007.

Green, Emily K. *Healthy Eating* (The New Food Guide Pyramid). Minneapolis: Bellwether Media, 2006.

Schlosser, Eric, and Wilson, Charles. *Chew On This: Everything You Don't Want to Know About Fast Food*. New York: Houghton Mifflin, 2006.

Schuh, Mari C. *Healthy Snacks* (Healthy Eating with MyPyramid). Mankato, MN: Capstone Press, 2006.

Taylor-Butler, Christine. *Food Allergies* (A True Book™: Health and the Human Body). New York: Children's Press, 2008.

Taylor-Butler, Christine. *Food Safety* (A True Book™: Health and the Human Body). New York: Children's Press, 2008.

Organizations and Web Sites

MyPyramid for Kids
www.mypyramid.gov/kids
The USDA Web site on the new food pyramid.

Nutrition Explorations
www.nutritionexplorations.org/kids/nutrition-pyramid.asp
Explore the interactive food pyramid.

Cool Food Planet
www.coolfoodplanet.org/gb/kidz
Read tips for healthful eating and keeping fit.
Try the nutrition quiz.

Place to Visit

ARS National Visitor Center
Powder Mill Road
Beltsville, MD 20705
301-504-9403
www.ars.usda.gov/is/nvc
Tour the visitor center for the
USDA's Agricultural Research
Service, where you can
learn about food science
and nutrition.

Important Words

anemia (uh-NEE-mee-uh) – a condition in which the iron level in the blood is too low to transport sufficient oxygen to the cells

calcium (KAL-see-uhm) – a mineral often found in foods

calorie (KAL-uh-ree) – a unit of measure of the energy contained in a food

carbohydrate (kar-boh-HYE-drate) – a nutrient in food that provides the body with energy

cholesterol (kuh-LESS-tuh-rol) – a kind of fatty substance found in animal tissues

diabetes (dye-uh-BEE-teez) – a disease in which there is too much glucose (sugar) in the blood

fiber (FYE-bur) – edible plant material that is not digestible by the body

hormone (HOR-mohn) – a chemical made in the body that controls body processes and affects the way a person grows

insulin (IN-suh-luhn) – a hormone that controls the amount of glucose (sugar) in the blood

protein (PROH-teen) – a kind of substance used by the body for many things, including growth and repair of tissue

Index

Page numbers in **bold** indicate illustrations

About the Author

Christine Taylor-Butler lives in Kansas City, Missouri, with her husband and two daughters. A native of Ohio, she is the author of more than 40 books for children. She holds a B.S. degree in both Civil Engineering and Art and Design from the Massachusetts Institute of Technology in Cambridge, MA. Other books by Ms. Taylor-Butler in the True Book Health and the Human Body series include: *Food Allergies*, *Food Safety*, *The Circulatory System*, *The Respiratory System*, *The Digestive System*, and *The Nervous System*.

PHOTOGRAPHS: Big Stock Photo (Volkan Ersoy, p. 9; Julian Rovagnati Martinez, p. 28); Getty Images (p. 8; p. 10; p. 29; p. 36; p. 38); Health Canada: Canada's Food Guide (food rainbow, p. 18); Ingram Image Library (vegetables, cover; carrots, back cover); iStockPhoto.com (Devon Yu, p. 40; © Diane Diederich, milk, cover; iofoto, p. 20; © Lewis Wright, p. 6; Michael Gray, p. 31; Vinko Murko, p. 5); Masterfile (p. 33); Photodisc (fruits, poultry and bread, cover; pumpkin, back cover; p. 24 Photolibrary (p. 34); Stock Central/age fotostock (types of oils, p. 17; p. 27); Stock.XCHNG (p. 5; p. 22); Stockxpert (p. 11; pp. 16–17; rice jar, p. 22; bread loaf, p. 23; p. 25; p. 30; p. 32; p. 37; p. 41); Tranz/Corbis (p. 3; p. 12; p. 42). All other images property of Weldon Owen Education.